From Your Friends At **The MAILBOX®**

OCTOBER

A MONTH OF REPRODUCIBLES AT YOUR FINGERTIPS!

Grades 2–3

Project Editor:
Amy Erickson

Editor:
Darcy Brown

Writers:
Rebecca Brudwick, Stacie Stone Davis,
Allison White Haynes, Cynthia Holcomb, Nicole Iacovazzi,
Njeri Jones, Mary Lester, Kimberly Taylor

Art Coordinator:
Clevell Harris

Artists:
Jennifer Tipton Bennett, Teresa Davidson, Nick Greenwood,
Clevell Harris, Susan Hodnett, Sheila Krill, Rob Mayworth,
Kimberly Richard, Rebecca Saunders

Cover Artist:
Jennifer Tipton Bennett

www.themailbox.com

©1999 by THE EDUCATION CENTER, INC.
All rights reserved.
ISBN #1-56234-276-2

Manufactured in the United States
10 9 8 7 6 5 4 3 2

Table Of Contents

Name _____

October Free Time

Monday	Tuesday	Wednesday	Thursday	Friday
Make a card for someone you care about on Care-acter Day, October 1. Don't forget to give the person a big hug! 	Charlie Brown®, Snoopy®, and the gang first appeared in newspapers on October 2, 1950. Write and illustrate your own version of the PEANUTS® comic strip.	It's the Month Of The Dinosaur! Think about what our environment was like long ago. Draw a prehistoric scene to share with a friend.	October 4 is Ten-Four Day! The words "ten-four" are used by radio operators to say "yes." Write the numerals "10-4" on a small piece of paper. Tape the paper onto your desk as a reminder to use that code for "yes" today. **10·4**	Write a letter to your local post office suggesting a new stamp design during National Stamp Collecting Month. Be creative!
On October 7, 1986, the rose was officially chosen as our national flower. What's your favorite flower? Write a poem about it.	Columbus Day is annually observed on the second Monday in October. Columbus landed in the New World on October 12, 1492. Pretend you are Columbus and write a diary entry for that day.	The second full week in October is National School Lunch Week! Make a card to thank your cafeteria staff for preparing healthful meals.	Construction began on the White House on October 13, 1792. Draw a picture of this important building. 	October is National Pasta Month. On a sheet of paper, make a list of dishes made with noodles. Circle your favorites on the list.
National School Bus Safety Week is in October. Pretend you're a bus driver and create a poster of bus safety rules.	October 15 is National Grouch Day! Write a paragraph about a grouchy storybook character. 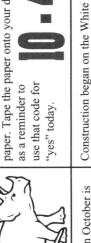	Dictionary Day is celebrated on October 16 in honor of Noah Webster, who put together the first American dictionaries. Look up word *dictionary* and write its definition.	Take a minute of your time to remember National Clock Month. Clocks not only tell time but also decorate homes. Draw a picture of a fancy new clock.	Recognize National Dessert Month in October by listing your top ten favorite desserts.
National Forest Products Week celebrates our forests' resources. Draw five different items in your classroom that come from trees. 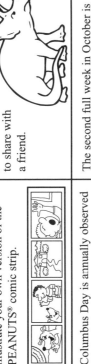	It's National Popcorn Poppin' Month! Write a great recipe for a new popcorn snack. 	Celebrate Make A Difference Day on the fourth Saturday in October. Write about a time that you helped at school or in your neighborhood.	How many different number sentences can you write for 20? Write them on a sheet of paper, then circle your favorite. $10+10=20$ $50-30=20$ $5+5+5+5=20$	October 31, 1941, marked the end of work on the national monument, Mount Rushmore. Find and write three interesting facts about this monument. 

Note To The Teacher: Have each student staple a copy of this page inside a file folder. Direct students to store their completed work in their folders.

October
Events And Activities For The Family

Directions: Select at least one activity below to complete as a family by the end of October.
(Challenge: See if your family can complete all three activities.)

The Popcorn Institute
401 N. Michigan Avenue
Chicago, IL 60611-4267

National Popcorn Poppin' Month

To kick off National Popcorn Poppin' Month, make yourselves a buttery popcorn snack! To learn more about this "a-maize-ing" food, read *The Popcorn Book* by Tomie dePaola (Scholastic Book Services, 1978) or write a family letter to The Popcorn Institute requesting more information about popcorn. Don't be surprised when many intriguing facts about this wholesome food pop up!

Make A Difference Day

The fourth Saturday in October is National Make A Difference Day. Team up with your family members to make a positive impact on your community! Select a public service project in which your family can participate, such as volunteering at a local homeless shelter or spending time with older citizens at a convalescent home. Helping neighbors with fall yard work and working with Habitat For Humanity to build homes for low-income families are good ideas, too. Bonding together to make a difference will be a rewarding family experience!

Family History Month

Work together to create an album of precious family memories during October, Family History Month. Have each family member make two or more pages to contribute to the album. To make a page, each family member gathers photos or draws small illustrations of his or her most memorable family experiences; then he or she mounts the pictures onto a sheet of construction paper. Next, each member adds captions and personalizes the page as desired. After each family member has completed his or her pages, create an album cover. Compile the pages with the cover, hole-punch the top of the pages and cover, and fasten them together with a length of ribbon. This picture-perfect album will be a valuable treasure to share with friends and relatives!

The Jones Family Album

It's Harvesttime!

This bountiful crop of skill-building fun is just ripe for the picking!

Join The Barn Dance!

Treat students to toe-tappin' fun with this creative barnyard activity. Read aloud *Barn Dance!* by Bill Martin, Jr. (Henry Holt And Company, Inc.; 1988). Then have each student select an animal from the story and use its name to create an alliterative dance name, such as the Piggie Polka or the Goat Gallop. Ask each student to illustrate and label his idea on a sheet of drawing paper. Display youngsters' completed work on a bulletin board titled "It's A Harvest Hoedown!" Then, using the display as a reference, ask students to determine an answer to this question: "If there are [number] dancing feet at the hoedown, what animals could there be?" Have each youngster write and illustrate his answer, then share his work. Students may be surprised to learn that this math problem has many correct answers!

A Little Bird Told Me

This literature-based activity is a great springboard for a discussion about making dreams a reality. Read aloud *The Harvest Birds: Los Pájaros De La Cosecha* (Children's Book Press, 1995). This bilingual folktale tells the story of Juan, who dreams of having his own land. With lots of hard work and the help of the harvest birds, he makes his dream come true. At the conclusion of the story, discuss with youngsters how Juan's determination and farming techniques resulted in a bountiful harvest. Then invite each student to tell what she would plant if she had her own land. Have each youngster draw and color a picture of her dream garden. Then display students' pictures on a bulletin board decorated with harvest bird cutouts and titled "Harvest Dreams."

Piggie Polka

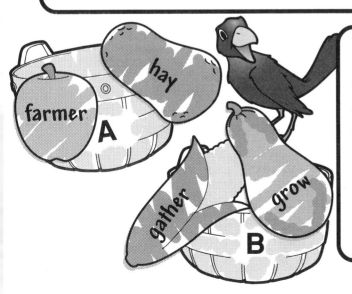

Harvesting Baskets Of Skills

Students will have bushels of fun with this small-group sorting activity! In advance, make four copies of page 7. On each of eight vegetable patterns, write a different harvesttime noun. Program the remaining vegetables with verbs. Divide students into small groups. Give each group a construction-paper copy of page 6 and of each programmed sheet. Have youngsters lightly color and cut out the baskets and vegetables. Then direct each group to place the vegetables with nouns on basket *A* and those with verbs on basket *B*. Verify students' work; then have them scramble the vegetables and sort them by another attribute, such as syllables. For even more sorting fun, program the vegetables with odd and even numerals or long- and short-vowel words.

5

Patterns
Use with "Harvesting Baskets Of Skills" on page 5.

Pumpkin Patch Pairs

Read each sentence.
Use the word banks to find the antonym of each boldfaced word.
Write the antonym in the blank.
Color the picture.

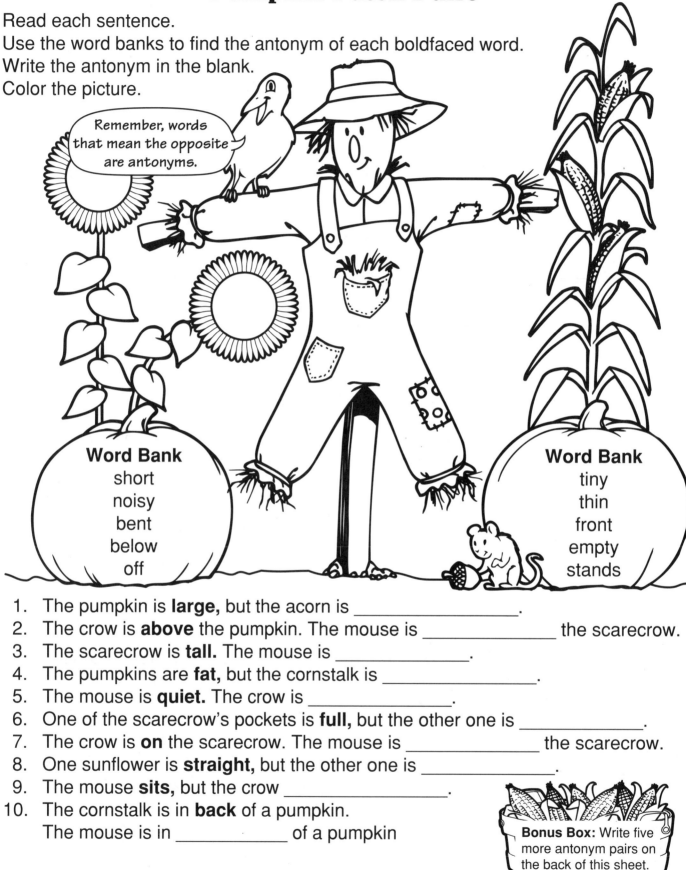

Remember, words
that mean the opposite
are antonyms.

Word Bank
short
noisy
bent
below
off

Word Bank
tiny
thin
front
empty
stands

1. The pumpkin is **large,** but the acorn is _____.
2. The crow is **above** the pumpkin. The mouse is _____ the scarecrow.
3. The scarecrow is **tall.** The mouse is _____.
4. The pumpkins are **fat,** but the cornstalk is _____.
5. The mouse is **quiet.** The crow is _____.
6. One of the scarecrow's pockets is **full,** but the other one is _____.
7. The crow is **on** the scarecrow. The mouse is _____ the scarecrow.
8. One sunflower is **straight,** but the other one is _____.
9. The mouse **sits,** but the crow _____.
10. The cornstalk is in **back** of a pumpkin.
    The mouse is in _____ of a pumpkin

Bonus Box: Write five
more antonym pairs on
the back of this sheet.

Name _____

In The Cornfield

Read each problem.
Write the answer in the blank.
Cross out each answer on the basket as you use it.

1. Carl Crow ate 11 ears of corn.
   Crabby Crow ate 7 ears of corn.
   How many more ears did Carl
   eat? _____

2. There are 8 crows in the cornfield.
   Four more crows will join them.
   How many crows will there be in
   all? _____

3. One stalk of corn has 6 ears.
   Another stalk has 5 ears and
   another one has 3 ears.
   How many ears are there in all?

   _____

4. There are 4 pumpkins in a row.
   There are 4 rows.
   How many pumpkins are there
   altogether? _____

5. Farmer Fred picked a lot of
   apples this week.
   He picked 7 baskets on Thursday
   and 5 baskets on Friday.
   He picked 8 baskets on Saturday.
   How many baskets did he pick in
   all? _____

6. The scarecrow chased away 13
   crows in the morning.
   He chased away 6 crows in the
   afternoon.
   How many crows were chased
   altogether? _____

7. The crows will eat 4 ears of corn
   for breakfast.
   They will eat 6 ears for lunch and
   7 ears for dinner.
   How many ears will they eat in
   all? _____

8. There are 5 stalks of corn in each
   row.
   There are 3 rows.
   How many stalks are there
   altogether? _____

9. The scarecrow has 13 buttons on
   his shirt.
   He has 4 buttons on his pants.
   How many more buttons are on
   his shirt? _____

10. Farmer Fred will plant 16 rows of
    corn.
    He will plant 9 rows of pumpkins.
    How many more rows of corn will
    he have? _____

7   12   15   4   19
16   9   20   14   17

Sammy Scarecrow

Follow the directions to make Sammy Scarecrow.
Make a check mark in each box after you complete the step.

☐ 1. Color the hat brown.

☐ 2. Color the shirt and sleeves red.

☐ 3. Color the pant legs blue.

☐ 4. Color the rest of Sammy with any colors you choose.

☐ 5. Cut out all of the pieces.

☐ 6. Glue piece **A** to piece **B**.

☐ 7. Glue piece **C** to piece **D**.

☐ 8. Glue piece **E** to piece **F**.

☐ 9. Glue piece **G** to piece **H**.

☐ 10. Glue piece **I** to piece **J**.

☐ 11. Glue Sammy onto another sheet of paper.

☐ 12. Draw and color a pumpkin patch for Sammy.

head

body

legs

arms

Bonus Box: Write a story about Sammy on another sheet of paper.

©1999 The Education Center, Inc. • *October Monthly Reproducibles* • Grades 2–3 • TEC961

Note To The Teacher: Each student will need a sheet of construction paper, crayons, scissors, and glue to complete this activity.

Oktoberfest

Travel with students to Germany with this *wunderbar* Oktoberfest unit!

Next Stop, Germany

Begin your visit abroad by sharing with youngsters this Oktoberfest information.

Oktoberfest began in 1810 as a wedding reception in a Munich meadow. King Maximillian hosted the reception to celebrate the marriage of his son, Prince Ludwig, to Princess Therese. The celebration featured horse races. The king decided to make the celebration an annual event, and the meadow was named *Theresienwiese* in honor of Princess Therese.

Now Oktoberfest is a 16-day gala that ends on the first Sunday in October. Oktoberfest is celebrated in a variety of ways in both Germany and the United States. There are rides for children, such as roller coasters and merry-go-rounds. Contests are held, bands play, and lots of traditional German foods are served, too.

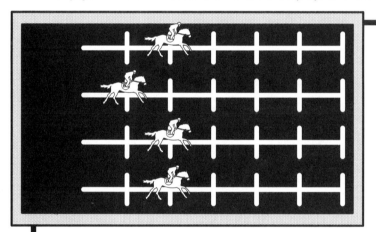

The Race Is On!

This team math game will be a race to the finish! Duplicate on construction paper a class supply of the game cards on page 12. Also, make two copies of the patterns on page 13 to make a total of four racehorses. Cut apart the game cards and program each one with a different math problem. Place the prepared cards in a stack. Label one horse with each of the following letters: *A, B, C,* and *D.* Then cut out and laminate the prepared horses. On the chalkboard, draw a simple racetrack as shown. Explain to students that horse races were held during the first Oktoberfest.

Tell students that they will play a *math* horse race game. Divide students into four teams. Tape a horse cutout for each team on a starting line.

To play, take the top racehorse card and read aloud the problem to the first player on Team A. If he answers correctly, his team's horse advances to the next space and the card is placed in a discard pile. If the answer is incorrect, the horse is not moved and the card is returned to the bottom of the stack. Play continues with the remaining teams and players in a like manner until a team crosses the finish line. (Shuffle and restack the game cards as necessary.) If desired, serve pretzels to celebrate a job well done.

Come One, Come All!

Try this Oktoberfest brochure project with your young travelers! Share with students the information about Oktoberfest on this page (see "Next Stop, Germany"). If desired, provide students with resource materials to research additional information. To make a brochure, each student trifolds a sheet of drawing paper as shown. On his brochure cover, he writes "Oktoberfest." Then he personalizes and decorates the cover as desired. Next he opens his brochure and visually divides it on the fold lines. In the first section, the student summarizes and illustrates the history of Oktoberfest. In the second and third sections, he writes about Oktoberfest events and other festival information; then he illustrates his work. Not only will students learn a lot about Oktoberfest, they'll improve their abilities to summarize, too!

Game Cards

Use with "The Race Is On!" on page 11.

Merry-Go-Round Fun

Read each word.
Color its horse.
Use the color code.

Color Code:
soft *g* like in **Germany**: blue
hard *g* like in **go**: purple
soft *c* like in **city**: yellow
hard *c* like in **car**: green

Bonus Box: Choose four of the words. Write a sentence with each word on the back of this sheet.

Name _____

Pretzel Problems

Pretzels are one of the most popular Oktoberfest foods.
Solve each problem.
Then color the pretzel with the matching answer.

A.
$$\begin{array}{r} 4 \\ + 8 \\ \hline \end{array}$$

B.
$$\begin{array}{r} 7 \\ + 7 \\ \hline \end{array}$$

C.
$$\begin{array}{r} 16 \\ + 2 \\ \hline \end{array}$$

D.
$$\begin{array}{r} 9 \\ + 7 \\ \hline \end{array}$$

E.
$$\begin{array}{r} 7 \\ + 8 \\ \hline \end{array}$$

F.
$$\begin{array}{r} 9 \\ + 6 \\ \hline \end{array}$$

G.
$$\begin{array}{r} 5 \\ + 8 \\ \hline \end{array}$$

H.
$$\begin{array}{r} 8 \\ + 8 \\ \hline \end{array}$$

I.
$$\begin{array}{r} 7 \\ + 6 \\ \hline \end{array}$$

J.
$$\begin{array}{r} 5 \\ + 9 \\ \hline \end{array}$$

K.
$$\begin{array}{r} 4 \\ + 14 \\ \hline \end{array}$$

L.
$$\begin{array}{r} 6 \\ + 9 \\ \hline \end{array}$$

M.
$$\begin{array}{r} 9 \\ + 9 \\ \hline \end{array}$$

N.
$$\begin{array}{r} 11 \\ + 7 \\ \hline \end{array}$$

O.
$$\begin{array}{r} 8 \\ + 9 \\ \hline \end{array}$$

Bonus Box: There are eight students. Each student has two pretzels. How many pretzels are there in all? Solve the problem on the back of this sheet.

Oktoberfest: Then And Now

Read the paragraph.

Prince Ludwig married Princess Therese in October 1810. The king had a wedding celebration for them. There were horse races in the meadow during the celebration. The king decided to have the races every year. Then the meadow was named after the princess. Now Oktoberfest celebrations have parades, rides for children, and lots of food.

Look at the words in the paragraph.

1. Draw a box around the words that tell when the wedding celebration was held.
2. Underline a synonym for *field*. (Remember, a synonym is a word that means the same.)
3. Who was the meadow named after? Circle the name of the person.

Draw and color an Oktoberfest picture timeline.

Fire Prevention Week

What is the hottest month of the year? October! That's when Fire Prevention Week is observed. The first or second week in October has been set aside for fire safety education since 1925. Use this unit to ignite interest in fire safety and add spark to skills reinforcement!

Make Your Escape!

Teach youngsters safety rules for leaving a burning building with this hot idea. Share with students the escape plan shown. Then give each student a tagboard copy of page 18. Have each student write a different safety tip on each ladder rung. Next ask him to cut out the pattern pieces and cut Dalmation Dan's coat on the bold lines. Instruct him to fold the Dalmatian Dan cutout on the dotted line and carefully cut on the fold to make a narrow slit. Then have the student unfold the cutout and pull the ladder through the slit (see the illustration). Ask him to read his escape plan as he slides Dalmatian Dan up the ladder. To celebrate his fire safety knowledge, attach the student's Great Escape Award to his shirt with a safety pin.

Once outside, call 911.

Do not open a hot door!

Get out immediately!

Shout "Fire"

Stay low!

- Stay low. (*Clean air is close to the floor.*)

- Shout, "Fire!" (*Warn others.*)

- Get out immediately. (*Don't waste time looking for something.*)

- Do not open a hot door. (*Feel the door before opening it. If it's hot, find another exit.*)

- Once outside, call 911. (*Use a neighbor's phone.*)

ABC Rescue

Here's an alphabetizing challenge that's not too hot for *your* firefighters to handle! Give each student a copy of page 19. Have her alphabetize the words as directed. Then, instruct the student to cut out the hose at the bottom of her page and use a brad to attach it to Dalmatian Dan (see the illustration). Next have her rotate the hose to help Dan put out the fire. Now, that's a first-class firefighter!

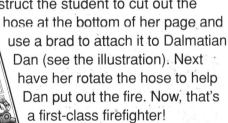

Hot Stuff

Heat up students' interest in fire safety with these red-hot books!

- *Fire Trucks* by Hope I. Marston (Dutton Children's Books, 1996)
- *Fire!* by Joy Masoff (Scholastic Inc., 1998)
- *Firehouse* by Katherine K. Winkleman (Walker Publishing Company, Inc.; 1994)

Patterns

Use with "Make Your Escape!" on page 17.

GREAT ESCAPE

Name

AWARD

ABC Rescue

Help the firefighters put out the blaze.
For each window, number the buckets to put the list in ABC order.
The first one has been done for you.

3 ax	bucket
1 aid	boots
2 alarm	best

rescue	spray
rope	smoky
rig	siren

pump	fire
pole	foam
protect	fumes
people	flames

chief	hack
captain	hydrant
crew	hose
company	helmet
clue	hunt

emergency	special
extinguisher	walkie-talkie
dalmatian	mask
ladder	safety
equipment	nozzle
break	work

Bonus Box: Circle ten words that name things firefighters might use to put out a fire.

©1999 The Education Center, Inc. • *October Monthly Reproducibles* • Grades 2–3 • TEC961 • Key p. 63

Rescuers In Action

Read the pages.

Cut out Dalmatian Dan, the cover, and the story pages. Write your name on
   the cover.

Stack the pages in the correct order. Place the cover on top of the stack.

Staple the booklet to Dan's helmet.

Firefighter _____ Name	The firefighters get on the truck quickly, and off it goes!	After the fire is out, firefighters clean and check their equipment.

Firefighters wait for the alarm to go off.

The firefighters return to the station to wait for another call.

When the alarm goes off, the firefighters stop what they are doing.

The firefighters fight the blaze with special equipment.

Place the booklet pages here.

National Metric Week

What better way to recognize National Metric Week—the first full week of October—than with an imaginary trip to Metric Land! These "meter-ific" ideas are just the ticket!

Jack's Journey

Prepare students for the journey to Metric Land with this interactive display. On an easily accessible bulletin board or wall, mount a simple castle-and-cloud cutout as shown. Next cut five or more different lengths of green yarn, each measuring a whole number of centimeters. Secure one end of each yarn length below the cloud, and the other end near the bottom of the display. Label each resulting beanstalk with a numeral, and title the display "Jack's Journey." Then share with students your favorite version of "Jack And The Beanstalk." Next give each student a copy of the ruler on page 22. Have her cut it out and glue it together where indicated. To use the display, a student measures each yarn beanstalk with her prepared ruler. She records and labels the measurements on a sheet of paper. Then the youngster determines the distance traveled if Jack went up beanstalk #1 and down beanstalk #3. She repeats this step with additional combinations of beanstalks. After students have completed their work, ask them to share their results in small groups.

Jack's Adventures In Metric Land

Fee-fi-fo-fum! Metric Land, here we come! Give youngsters loads of measurement practice with this booklet project featuring Jack and the giant. Duplicate a class supply of pages 22–24. Have each student cut out the ruler on page 22 and glue it together where indicated. (If the student completed "Jack's Journey" on this page, have him use his ruler from that activity.) To make a booklet, each student personalizes, colors, and cuts out a copy of the cover on page 22. Next he folds a 9" x 12" sheet of colored construction paper in half. Keeping the fold at the top, he glues his prepared cover onto the construction paper. Then he cuts apart the booklet pages on pages 23 and 24, stacks them in order, and staples them between his construction-paper covers (see the illustration on page 22). The student follows the directions on each page; then he colors the pages as desired. To provide additional measurement practice, ask each youngster to follow these directions:

Page 1: Draw a six-centimeter-tall beanstalk beside Jack's house.

Page 2: On the back of this page, draw, measure, and label two pencils—one for Jack and one for the giant.

Page 3: Draw a 10-centimeter-tall apple and a 15-centimeter-wide cake on the back of this page.

Page 4: One centimeter equals two kilometers on this map. Beside each of your measurements, write the matching number of kilometers.

Pattern And Booklet Cover

Use the pattern and booklet cover with "Jack's Adventures In Metric Land" on page 21.
Also use the pattern with "Jack's Journey" on page 21.

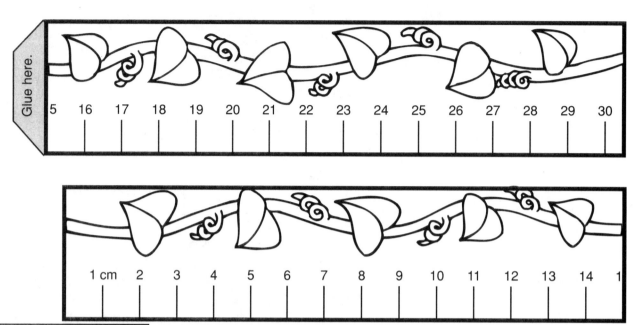

Project Sample

Jack's Adventures In Metric Land

Name _____

For Good Measure

Measure each bold line on Jack's house.
Write the length in its ▢.

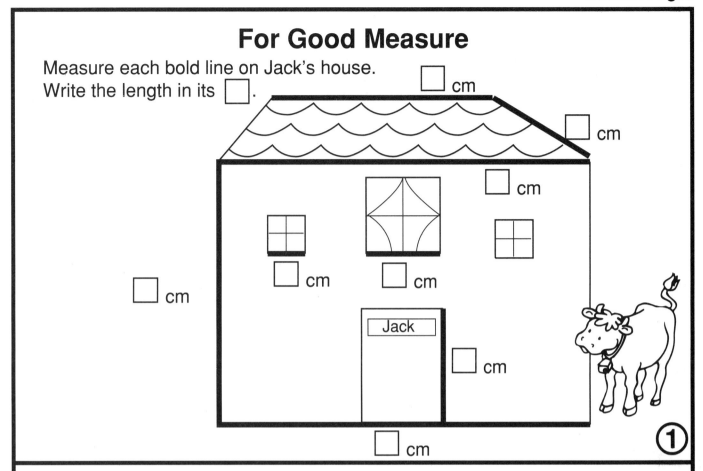

The Long And Short Of It

Measure each item between the ●s.
Write its length.
Find the difference between each pair of items. Write your answer.

Jack's Things	The Giant's Things	Differences
_____ cm	_____ cm	_____ cm
_____ cm	_____ cm	_____ cm
_____ cm	_____ cm	_____ cm
_____ cm	_____ cm	_____ cm ②

Note To The Teacher: Use with "Jack's Adventures In Metric Land" on page 21.

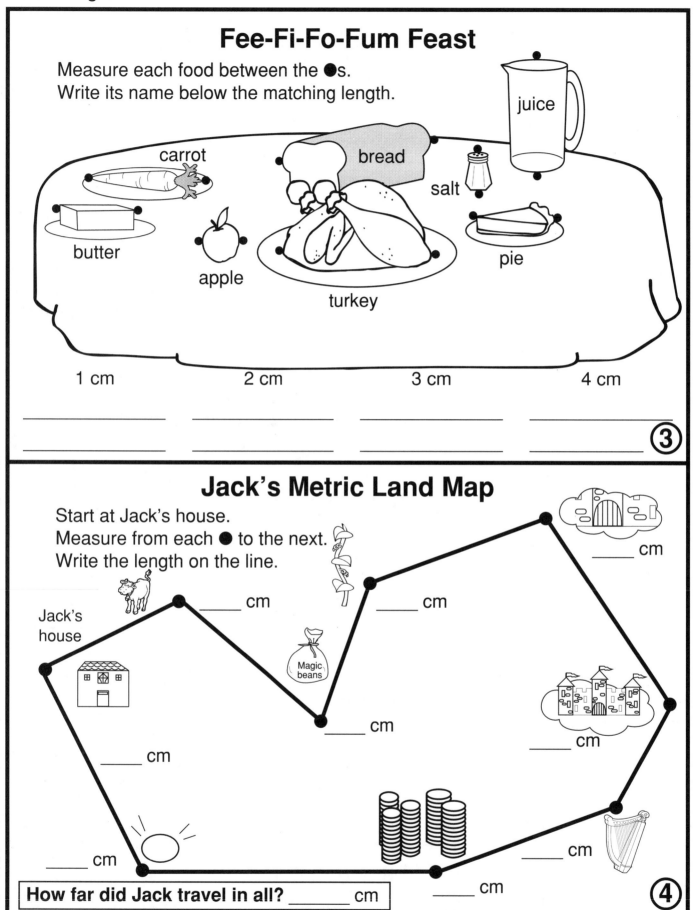

Fee-Fi-Fo-Fum Feast

Measure each food between the ●s.
Write its name below the matching length.

juice

carrot   bread

salt

butter

apple   pie

turkey

1 cm   2 cm   3 cm   4 cm

_____

_____

③

Jack's Metric Land Map

Start at Jack's house.
Measure from each ● to the next.
Write the length on the line.

_____ cm

Jack's
house

_____ cm

_____ cm

Magic
beans

_____ cm

_____ cm

_____ cm

_____ cm

_____ cm

_____ cm

How far did Jack travel in all? _____ cm

④

©1999 The Education Center, Inc. • *October Monthly Reproducibles* • Grades 2–3 • TEC961 • Key p. 63

24   **Note To The Teacher:** Use with "Jack's Adventures In Metric Land" on page 21.

Columbus Day

How can you make the second Monday in October an extraspecial Columbus Day? Easy! Use this collection of fact-filled activities to have fun *and* reinforce skills!

Sailing The Seas

Enjoy smooth sailing as you teach students about Columbus's most famous voyage with this hands-on map activity. Give each youngster a construction-paper copy of page 26 and ask student volunteers to read aloud the boxed sentences. Then give each student a craft stick and help him follow the steps below to complete the activity. Bon voyage!

Steps:
1. Cut out each sentence and glue it to the correct spot on the map.
2. Read and follow the directions at the bottom of the page. As you complete each step, make a check mark in its box.
3. Color and cut out the ships. Glue them to the tip of a craft stick.
4. Carefully slit the map on Columbus's route; then insert the craft stick through the slit as shown.
5. Read each sentence as you guide the ships along Columbus's route.

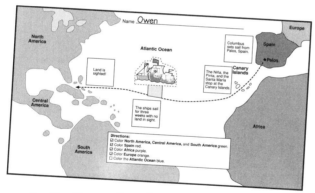

A-B-Sea Order

Ahoy, mateys! Here's a spiffy way to get your crew working on alphabetizing skills! Give a copy of page 28 and three brads to each student. On the lines provided, have him write each set of words in ABC order. Then instruct him to label the first ship "Santa María," the second ship "Niña," and the third ship "Pinta." Next have him cut out the ships and the waves on the bold lines. Ask the student to color the cutouts, being careful to leave the writing visible. Then have him fasten each ship to the waves above the corresponding list of words. There's no doubt about it—even your land-lubbers will have fun sailing *these* ships!

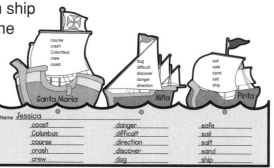

It's Your Life, Christopher Columbus!

Students will flip over this Christopher Columbus sequencing book! Give a 9" x 12" sheet of construction paper and a copy of page 27 to each student. Read the paragraphs with students and discuss which one should be first, second and so on. Then have each student follow the steps below to make a special flip book.

Steps:
1. Fold a sheet of construction paper in half widthwise. Fold it in half lengthwise; then fold it in half widthwise once more. Crease the folds.

2. Unfold the paper to reveal eight sections. Cut out the paragraphs on page 27; then glue them in order on the bottom four sections.

3. Cut out the cover patterns. Fold the construction-paper sheet in half lengthwise. Keeping the fold at the top, glue one cover cutout to each section (see the illustration). Then cut the cover along the creases to make four flaps. Open the flaps and illustrate each paragraph. Share your completed book with a friend.

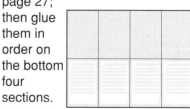

25

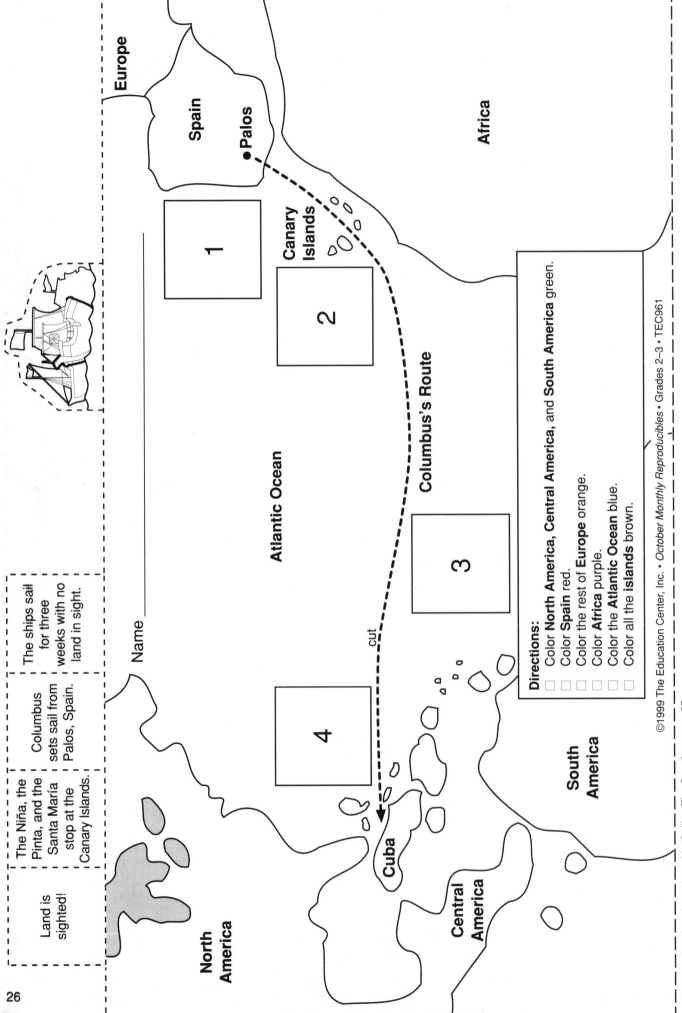

Europe

Spain

●Palos

Africa

1

Canary
Islands

2

Atlantic Ocean

Columbus's Route

cut

3

Name _____

4

The ships sail
for three
weeks with no
land in sight.

Columbus
sets sail from
Palos, Spain.

The Niña, the
Pinta, and the
Santa María
stop at the
Canary Islands.

Land is
sighted!

North
America

Cuba

Central
America

South
America

Directions:
- ☐ Color **North America, Central America,** and **South America** green.
- ☐ Color **Spain** red.
- ☐ Color the rest of **Europe** orange.
- ☐ Color **Africa** purple.
- ☐ Color the **Atlantic Ocean** blue.
- ☐ Color all the **islands** brown.

26

Columbus sailed to many places as he got older. He wanted to try a new route to the Indies to trade for gold and silk. The problem was that he needed ships to make the trip.

After almost ten years, Columbus got the ships he needed—the *Niña,* the *Pinta,* and the *Santa María.* Columbus set sail from Spain on August 3, 1492.

On October 12, 1492, Columbus landed in America. He thought he had landed in the Indies, near Japan. Columbus and his men explored nearby islands before they returned to Spain.

Christopher Columbus was born over 500 years ago. He was the oldest of five children. His father was a weaver. He grew up in Italy and lived by the Mediterranean Sea.

Ask me to read to you!

Name _____

The Life Of Columbus

Note To The Teacher: Use with "It's Your Life, Christopher Columbus!" on page 25.

Patterns

Use with "A-B-Sea Order" on page 25.

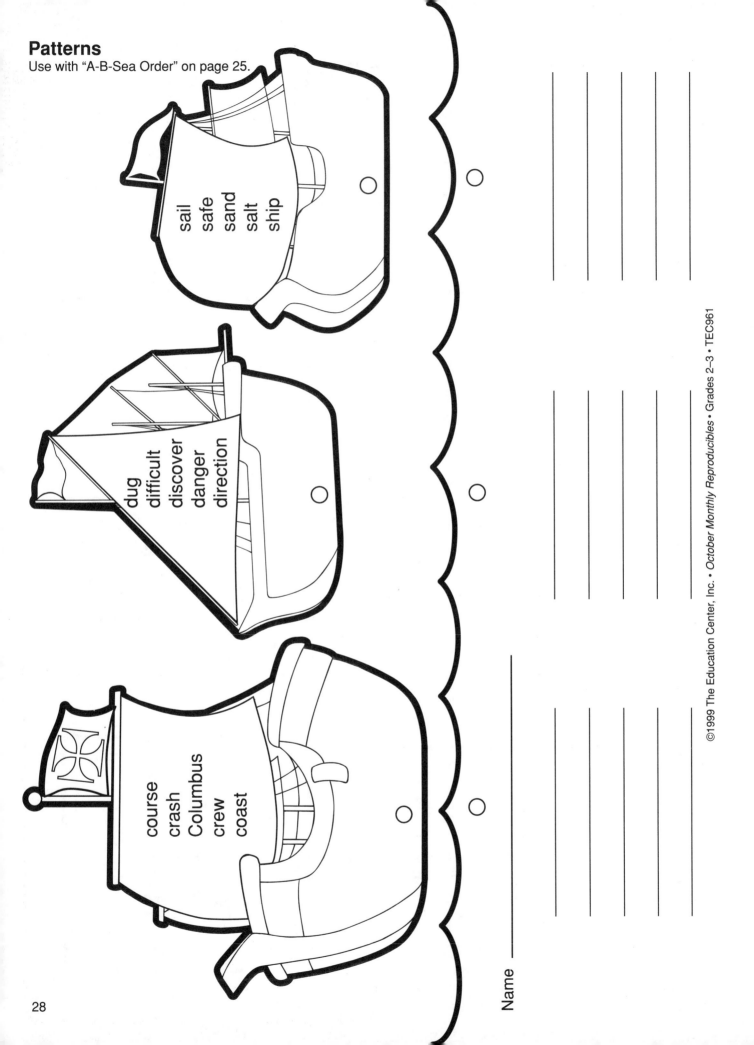

sail
safe
sand
salt
ship

dug
difficult
discover
danger
direction

course
crash
Columbus
crew
coast

Name _____

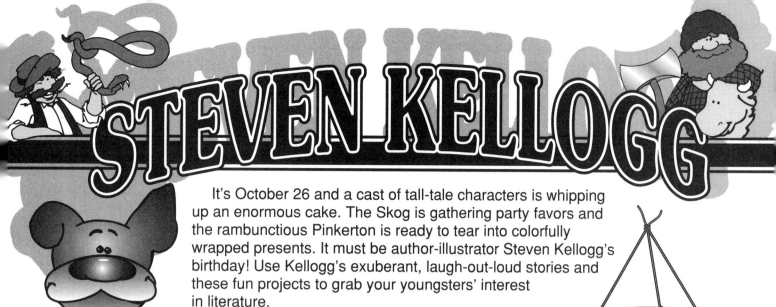

STEVEN KELLOGG

It's October 26 and a cast of tall-tale characters is whipping up an enormous cake. The Skog is gathering party favors and the rambunctious Pinkerton is ready to tear into colorfully wrapped presents. It must be author-illustrator Steven Kellogg's birthday! Use Kellogg's exuberant, laugh-out-loud stories and these fun projects to grab your youngsters' interest in literature.

Hanging Out With Pinkerton

Inspire your students to create a snazzy mobile *and* learn about story elements with Pinkerton's zany adventures. Read aloud to students *Pinkerton, Behave!* (Puffin Books, 1993), *Prehistoric Pinkerton* (Puffin Books, 1993), and *Tallyho, Pinkerton!* (Puffin Books, 1992). For each book, discuss with students the amusing events and their outcomes. Then use the directions shown to help each youngster make a Pinkerton mobile. Suspend students' completed mobiles from the ceiling for a very special salute to the hilarious Pinkerton!

Pinkerton Mobile

For each mobile you will need:
one construction-paper copy each of pages 30 and 31
one large paper plate
hole puncher
six large, unlined index cards
scissors
yarn
crayons

Directions:
1. Color and cut out each pattern on pages 30 and 31.
2. On the blank side of each title cutout, illustrate a scene from the corresponding book.
3. For each book, write about an amusing event on an index card. Flip over the card and illustrate it. In a similar manner, write and illustrate the outcome on another index card.
4. Write and complete the phrase "Pinkerton reminds me of…" on the back of the Pinkerton cutout.
5. Fold a paper plate in half. Just below the fold, hole-punch the plate once at the center, then unfold the plate.
6. Near the edge of the plate, punch three evenly spaced holes. Tie a length of yarn to each hole. Then tie the three lengths together as shown.
7. Hole-punch the top and bottom of each title pattern and event card. Also hole-punch the top of each outcome card and the Pinkerton cutout. Then assemble the mobile with yarn (see the illustration).

Colossal Collaboration

Improve students' communication and characterization skills with this crackerjack teamwork activity! Read aloud to students one of Steven Kellogg's tall-tale books, such as *Paul Bunyan* (Morrow Junior Books, 1985) or *Pecos Bill* (Morrow Junior Books, 1992). Then discuss with students the exaggerations in the story. Next give each student a copy of page 32. Have him create his own tall-tale character and write about his character on his sheet as indicated. Then collect the completed sheets and redistribute them so that each youngster has another student's paper. Instruct each student to carefully read about his classmate's character, then illustrate it on a sheet of drawing paper. Display each written sheet with its corresponding illustration on a colorful bulletin board titled "Tall-Tale Teamwork!" This exercise in clear communication will be an eye-opening experience, and that's no exaggeration!

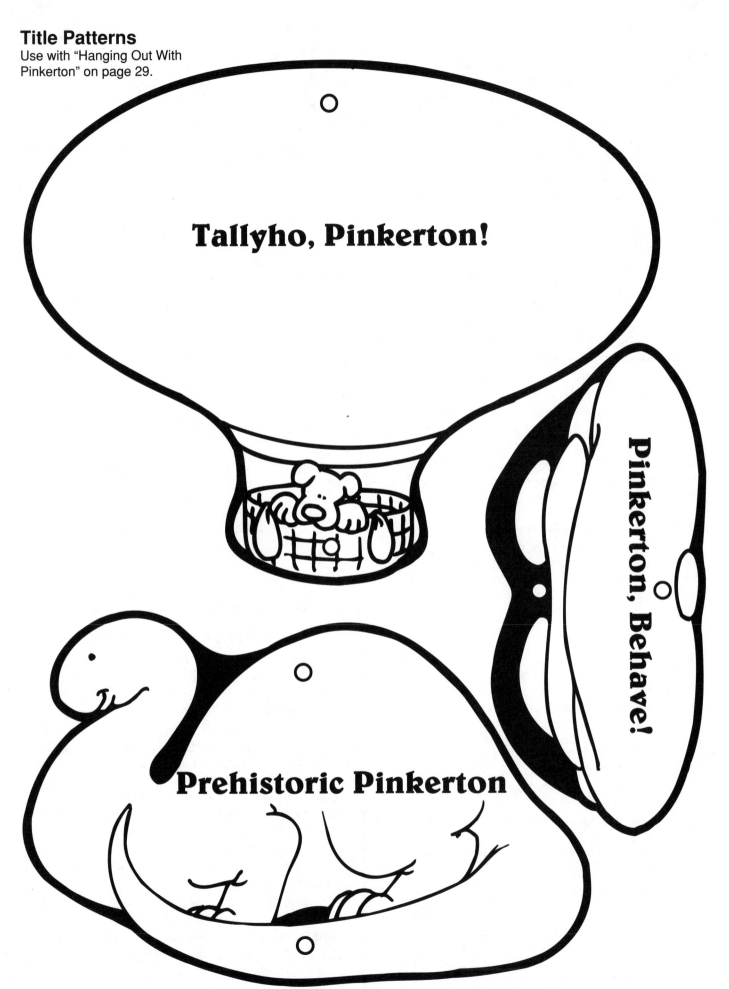

Tallyho, Pinkerton!

Pinkerton, Behave!

Prehistoric Pinkerton

Pinkerton Pattern And Bookmark

Use the Pinkerton pattern with "Hanging Out With Pinkerton" on page 29.

©1999 The Education Center, Inc. • *October Monthly Reproducibles* • Grades 2–3 • TEC961

Can I Keep Him? (Dial Books For Young Readers, 1971)

The Island Of The Skog (Puffin Books, 1993)

Jack And The Beanstalk (Morrow Junior Books, 1997)

Much Bigger Than Martin (NAL-Dutton, 1992)

The Three Little Pigs (Morrow Junior Books, 1997)

"Read these books written and illustrated by Steven Kellogg!"

Note To The Teacher: Duplicate the bookmark and distribute copies to students as desired.

Name_____

Tall-Tale Legend

Character's name: _____

What my character looks like: _____
_____
_____
_____

Where my character lives: _____
_____
_____
_____

My character's special abilities: _____
_____
_____
_____
_____
_____

Note to the artist:

Please show my character _____
_____
_____
_____
_____

SPIDERS, SPIDERS EVERYWHERE!

With this "spider-ific" collection of ideas and reproducibles, students will learn that arachnids are truly amazing!

Spectacular Spiders

Explore with students the fascinating world of spiders with this eye-opening research project. Share with youngsters the facts shown below; then ask them to re-search additional information about spiders. Give each student a copy of page 34 and have him write three facts about spiders on his sheet. Ask him to outline his spider's body with a black crayon, then color its head and legs. Next have the student cut out his spider. Display the completed arachnids on a bulletin board decorated with student-made webs and spiders (see "Web Weavers" on this page). Or have each student glue his spider onto a sheet of construction paper; then bind students' work between construc-tion-paper covers to make a class book.

Spider Facts

- There are about 40,000 different kinds of spiders.
- Most spiders have eight eyes, but they can't see very well.
- Some spiders can change color.
- The biggest kind of spider grows to be 11 inches wide.
- The smallest type of spider is so small that ten of them can fit on the end of a pencil.
- Spitting spiders do not make webs. They catch insects by spitting a sticky gum on them.
- The silk in a spider's web can stretch the length of a tennis court.

Web Weavers

A spider's work is never done! It often needs to make a new web because webs lose their stickiness and break easily. Have students try their hands at the intriguing art of web weaving with this fun project. For each student, hole-punch the edge of a paper plate at evenly spaced intervals. To weave her web, a youngster tapes to the back of her plate one end of a length of black yarn approximately eight feet long. Next she pulls the yarn through one of the holes to the front of the plate. She weaves the yarn to and from each hole as shown. (The yarn may be passed through a hole more than once.) If desired, she tapes additional lengths of yarn to the plate and weaves them into the web in a similar manner. After the student is satis-fied with her design, she pulls the yarn through a hole to the back of the plate, tapes it to the plate, and trims it. To make a spider for her web, she places four 3-inch lengths of black pipe cleaner in a stack. She fastens them together by tightly wrapping a two-inch black pipe cleaner around the center of them. The student positions the legs of the resulting spider as desired. Then she places it onto her web and bends the legs over the yarn to hold it in place.

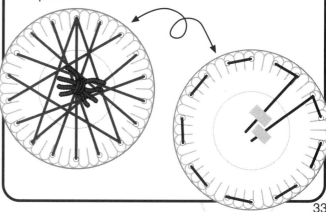

Note To The Teacher: Use with "Spectacular Spiders" on page 33.

Name_____

Spiders, Insects, Or Both?

Read the facts.
Write each fact in the correct area.

Facts	
A **spider** has • eight legs • two body parts (an *abdomen* and a *cephalothorax*) • jointed legs • no feelers or wings • a hard skeleton covering its body	An **insect** has • six legs • three body parts (an *abdomen, a thorax,* and a *head*) • jointed legs • feelers and wings (some insects) • a hard skeleton covering its body

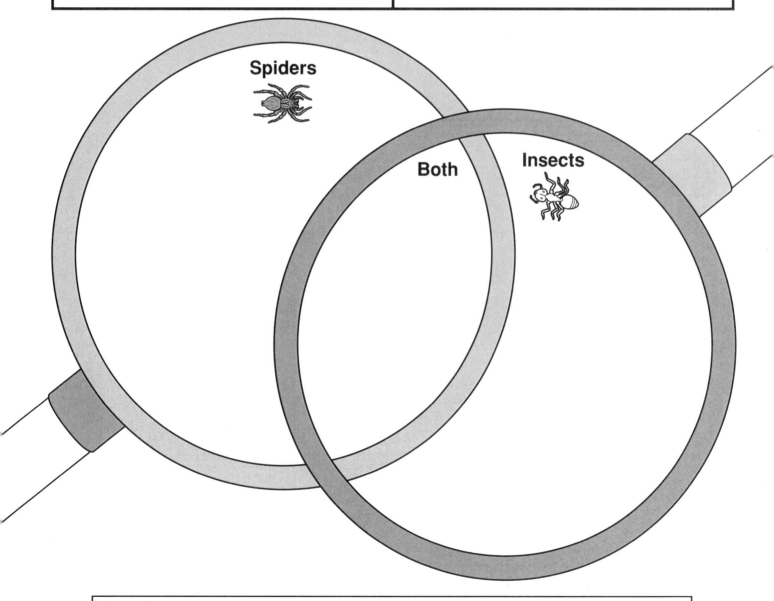

Bonus Box: On the back of this sheet, draw a spider and an insect. Use the facts above to help you.

Name_____

Spider Sprints

These spiders are getting ready to have a race.
Help them line up.
For each row, write the numerals in order from
    the lowest to the highest.

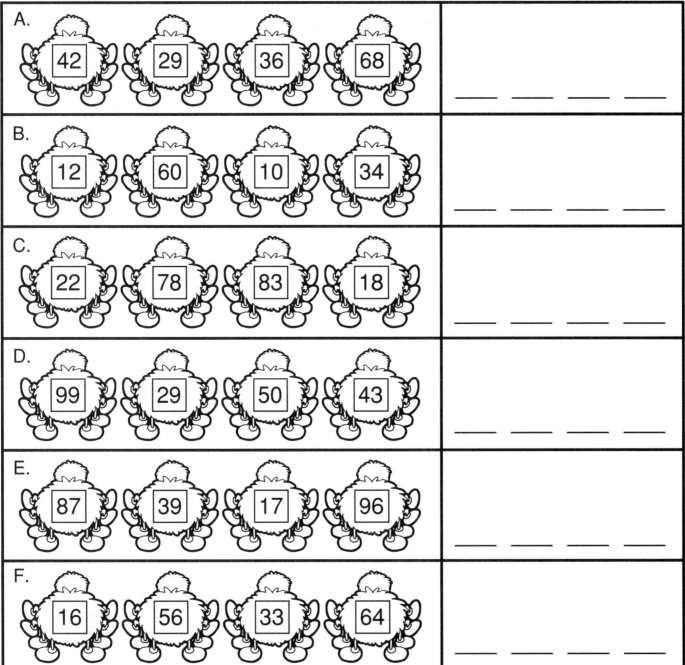

A. 42 29 36 68   ___ ___ ___ ___

B. 12 60 10 34   ___ ___ ___ ___

C. 22 78 83 18   ___ ___ ___ ___

D. 99 29 50 43   ___ ___ ___ ___

E. 87 39 17 96   ___ ___ ___ ___

F. 16 56 33 64   ___ ___ ___ ___

Bonus Box: On the back of this sheet, write six different numerals between 1 and 100. Ask a classmate
to write them in order from the lowest to the highest.

HALLOWEEN

This "boo-tiful" collection of ideas and reproducible activities is sure to scare up plenty of Halloween fun!

Monster Tales

Spark your youngsters' creative-writing skills with these spooky spectators! Give each student a copy of page 38. Instruct her to color and cut out a set of facial features and the pair of hands. Have her glue the features onto a nine-inch paper plate to make a monster face. While the glue dries, give each student a copy of page 39 and have her write a story about her monster. Then ask each youngster to color the rest of her monster's face and glue the hand patterns to the top of her story. Finally, have her staple her sheet to the paper-plate face (see the illustration). Count on these fearful, funny stories to be a Halloween hit!

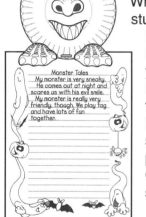

"Spook-tacular" Characters

You can be sure that your little goblins won't boo this character-analysis activity! To begin, read aloud *The Teeny Tiny Ghost* by Kay Winters (HarperCollins Publishers, Inc.; 1997) or your favorite ghost story. Then have each student make a paper ghost. To make a ghost, each youngster traces a stockinged foot on a 9" x 12" sheet of white construction paper, then cuts out his tracing. Next he turns his foot cutout upside down and writes on it five or more of the character's traits, as shown. The student adds features to his ghost to resemble the book character; then he glues the paper ghost onto a 9" x 12" sheet of black construction paper. Display the completed projects on a bulletin board covered with yellow paper and titled " 'Spook-tacular' Characters."

Crunchy Creepy-Crawlies

Motivate your youngsters to spin a web of spider facts! Tell students that each of them will earn ingredients to make an edible spider. Provide students with nonfiction spider books such as the ones shown below. Then have each student research and write eight facts about spiders. For each fact he writes, give the student a pretzel to use for the Creepy-Crawly recipe on this page. After earning eight pretzel-stick legs, help each student make his "arach-tacular" snack!

Notable Nonfiction

- *I Didn't Know That Spiders Have Fangs: And Other Amazing Facts About Arachnids* by Claire Llewellyn (Aladdin Books Ltd., 1997)
- *I Wonder Why Spiders Spin Webs: And Other Questions About Creepy Crawlies* by Amanda O'Neill and Paul Hillyard (Kingfisher, 1995)
- *The Spider* by Sabrina Crewe (Raintree Steck-Vaughn Publishers, 1998)
- *Tarantulas* by Conrad J. Storad (Lerner Publications Company, 1998)

Creepy-Crawly
(Makes one creepy-crawly.)

You'll need:
1 JET-PUFFED® toasted coconut marshmallow
8 pretzel sticks
2 mini chocolate chips
1 squeezable container of chocolate syrup
1 small paper plate

Lightly squeeze chocolate syrup onto the paper plate to make a spiderweb design. Insert four pretzel sticks into each side of the marshmallow. Press the chocolate chips into the marshmallow for eyes. Then place the spider on the chocolate web. Enjoy!

37

Note To The Teacher: Use with "Monster Tales" on page 37.

Name _____

Meet The Count!

Count! Count! Count!
Count by twos, threes, or fives.
Write a numeral in each blank to
complete the pattern.

A. 10, ___, ___, ___, 30, ___, ___, ___, ___

B. 6, 9, ___, ___, ___, 21, ___, ___, ___

C. 8, ___, ___, ___, 16, ___, ___, ___, ___

D. 18, ___, ___, ___, 30, ___, ___, ___, ___

E. 45, ___, ___, ___, ___, 70, ___, ___, ___

F. 34, ___, ___, ___, 42, ___, ___, ___, ___

G. 40, ___, ___, ___, ___, 50, ___, ___, ___

H. 30, ___, ___, ___, 42, ___, ___, ___, ___

If you counted by twos, draw a circle in front of the row.
If you counted by threes, draw a square in front of the row.
If you counted by fives, draw a triangle in front of the row.

Bonus Box: On the back of this sheet, write from 0 to 100 by twos. Then write from 0 to 100 by fives.

©1999 The Education Center, Inc. • *October Monthly Reproducibles* • Grades 2–3 • TEC961 • Key p. 64

Witches' Brew

Write *ch*, *sh*, *th*, or *wh* in each blank to complete the word.

___ air	___ ort	___ isper	___ ade
___ ell	___ eels	___ ought	___ ain
___ ile	___ arm	___ out	___ arp
___ ing	___ iskers	___ ird	___ art

Complete each sentence with a word from the witches' brew.

1. The witch's hat has a _____ point.

2. Her voice is a low, creaky _____.

3. She calls her cat for the _____ time.

4. She pets the cat's _____, black fur.

5. She sits in an old rocking _____ all day.

6. There she sits _____ she waits for the moon to appear.

7. With a _____, she rides off into the night.

8. There's no need for _____ because the witch uses a broom.

Bonus Box: On the back of this sheet, illustrate the witch described by the sentences.

Name_____

"Spook-tacular" Subtraction

Read the subtraction rule in each box.
Follow the rule to write an answer in each box.
The first one has been done for you.

1.

Rule: Subtract 9			
12	16	18	14
3			

4.

Rule: Subtract 8			
12	16	11	13

2.

Rule: Subtract 7			
15	13	17	11

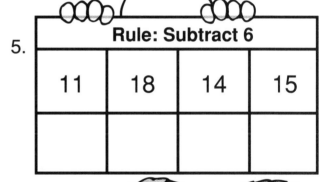

5.

Rule: Subtract 6			
11	18	14	15

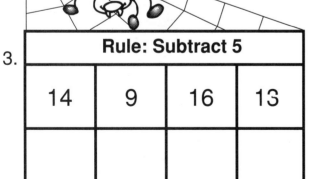

3.

Rule: Subtract 5			
14	9	16	13

6.

Rule: Subtract 11			
15	17	13	18

Bonus Box: On the back of this sheet, write a Halloween word problem. Ask a friend to solve it.

©1999 The Education Center, Inc. • *October Monthly Reproducibles* • Grades 2–3 • TEC961 • Key p. 64

NATIONAL PIZZA MONTH

Serve up this unit loaded with tempting learning activities during National Pizza Month in October.

Hold The Anchovies, Please!

Here's a survey idea with pizzazz! Give each student a copy of page 44. Read with youngsters the types of pizzas listed and have them predict which variety is the most popular among their friends and families. Instruct each student to ask each of ten people which of these pizzas is his favorite and then write his name on the corresponding pizza slice. After his survey is complete, have the student write at the bottom of his sheet three sentences about the information he collected. Ask students to share their results; then record all of the information on one large pizza cutout with tally marks as shown. Compare the results with students' predictions. Now that's a survey idea that really delivers!

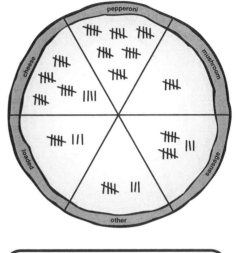

Poetry To Go

Spark students' creativity with this appetizing poetry-writing idea! Ask students to brainstorm words that describe pizza as you record their ideas on the chalkboard. Then give each student a copy of page 45. Have him imagine that a pizza has just been delivered to his house. Ask him to color the illustration to show the type of pizza he imagines. Next instruct him to complete the poem about his pizza, referring to the brainstormed adjectives as he works. Then ask the student to color the border and personalize his page as desired.

Pizzas With Personality

Put this get-better-acquainted project on your menu of bulletin-board ideas! Have each student color the edge of a paper plate brown to represent pizza crust. Ask her to color the remaining area red for sauce. Next instruct each youngster to cut from discarded magazines pictures of things she likes or activities she enjoys. Have her glue the pictures onto her paper plate pizza for toppings, then personalize her pizza as desired. Give each student an opportunity to present her completed pizza to the class. Cover a bulletin board with red and white checkered Con-Tact® paper or an inexpensive tablecloth. Title it "Pizzas With Personality"; then decorate the prepared bulletin board with the paper plate pizzas.

Name _____

Hold The Anchovies, Please!

Follow your teacher's directions.

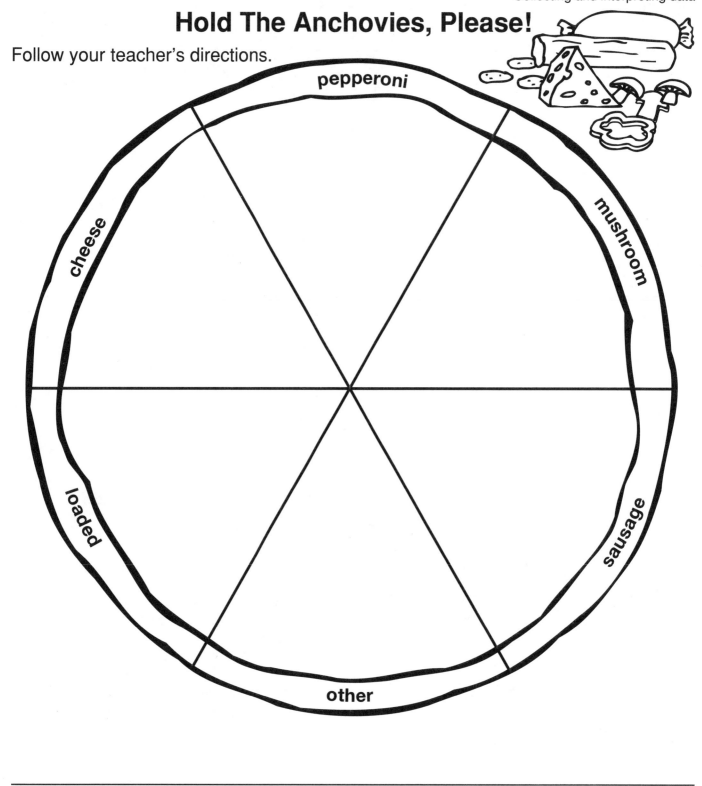

pepperoni

cheese

mushroom

loaded

sausage

other

_____

_____

_____

Note To The Teacher: Use with "Hold The Anchovies, Please!" on page 43.

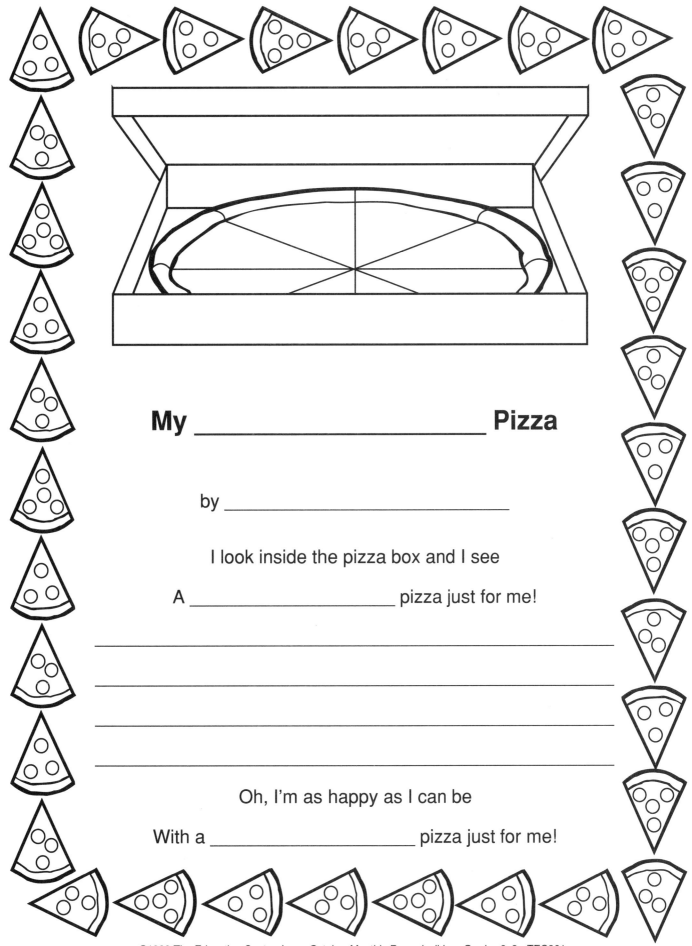

My _____ **Pizza**

by _____

I look inside the pizza box and I see

A _____ pizza just for me!

_____

_____

_____

_____

Oh, I'm as happy as I can be

With a _____ pizza just for me!

Note To The Teacher: Use with "Poetry To Go" on page 43.

At The Pizza Parlor

Read each sentence.
Write a synonym for the bold word(s).
Use the Word Bank.

1.  I would like a **small** piece of pizza, please. _____	2.  The waitress is **quick.** _____	3.  My napkin is **close to** my plate. _____
4.  I like pizza. I like soda, **too.** _____	5.  This pizza is too **big** for one person! _____	6.  Please do not **shout** in the restaurant. _____
7.  I ate the **entire** pizza! _____	8.  This pizza parlor is **excellent.** _____	9.  This pizza tastes **yummy!** _____

Word Bank

fast	delicious
large	near
yell	little
whole	also
fantastic	

Bonus Box: Choose five words from the Word Bank. On another sheet of paper, write a new sentence with each word.

Name _____

It's Pizza Time!

Read each clock.
Write the time below it.

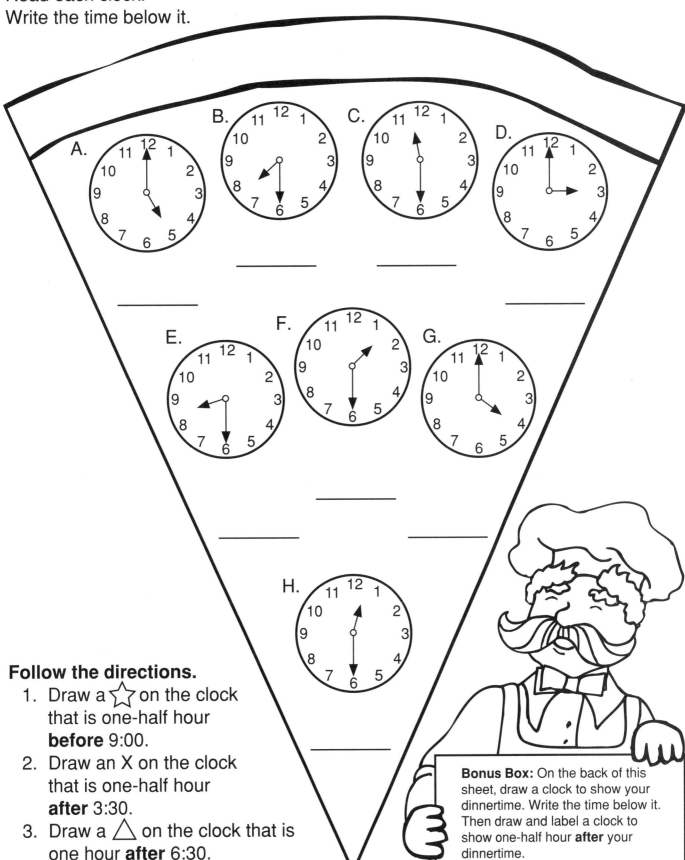

Follow the directions.

1. Draw a ☆ on the clock that is one-half hour **before** 9:00.
2. Draw an X on the clock that is one-half hour **after** 3:30.
3. Draw a △ on the clock that is one hour **after** 6:30.

Bonus Box: On the back of this sheet, draw a clock to show your dinnertime. Write the time below it. Then draw and label a clock to show one-half hour **after** your dinnertime.

Pizza Pie Math

Name _____

Study the pizzas in each row.
Write a matching fraction below each pizza.
The first one has been done for you.

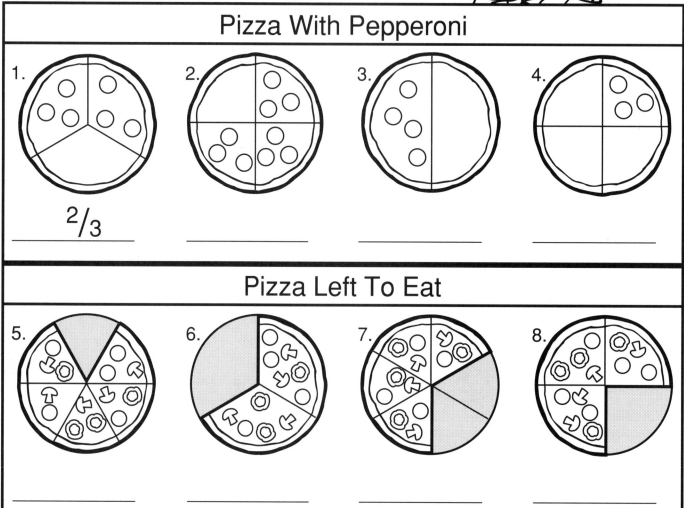

Pizza With Pepperoni

1. ___ 2/3 ___

2. _____

3. _____

4. _____

Pizza Left To Eat

5. _____

6. _____

7. _____

8. _____

Draw and color a pizza to match each fraction below.

Pizza With Mushrooms

9.

10.

11.

12.

___ 1/2 ___

___ 2/3 ___

___ 1/4 ___

___ 3/6 ___

National Popcorn Poppin' Month

Celebrate National Popcorn Poppin' Month in October with this "a-maize-ing" collection of fresh ideas!

Counting On Corn

Looking for convenient and inexpensive math manipulatives? If so, try unpopped kernels and popped corn. There are countless ways to use these corny manipulatives. Here are some ideas:

- Have students use popped corn for non-standard measurement practice.
- Ask youngsters to use unpopped kernels or popped corn to make geometric shapes or patterns.
- Place unpopped kernels in a clear container for an estimation activity.
- Give students sets of kernels for counting by 2s, 3s, 4s, or 5s.
- Provide unpopped kernels for youngsters to use when solving addition and subtraction problems.
- Have students practice dividing sets equally with unpopped kernels or popped corn.

Adjectives	Verbs	Nouns
yummy	pop	butter
fluffy	cook	treat
delicious	serve	snack
hot	eat	kernel
fresh	buy	box
salty	share	movie

A Sizzling Center

Serve up parts-of-speech practice with this mouthwatering center! Duplicate on white construction paper 3 popcorn boxes and 15 or more popcorn patterns from page 50. Cut out the patterns; then label one popcorn box for each of the following parts of speech: nouns, verbs, and adjectives. On each popcorn cutout, write a different noun, verb, or adjective (see the illustration for popcorn-related suggestions). Program the popcorn for self-checking by writing *N* for noun, *V* for verb, or *A* for adjective on the back of each cutout. Laminate the prepared cutouts if desired. Place the cutouts, pencils, and blank paper in a pan at a center.

To use the center, a student places the popcorn boxes on a work surface. Then she places each popcorn cutout on the corresponding box. She turns the cutouts over to check her work. Next she chooses a popcorn cutout from each box and writes a sentence using these three words. The student chooses additional cutouts and writes sentences with the corresponding words in a like manner. To vary this tantalizing center, program the popcorn cutouts with math problems and the boxes with the solutions. Or write a different word on each cutout and label the boxes with the matching number of syllables.

Patterns

Use with "A Sizzling Center" on page 49.

Corny Sentences

Cut apart the popcorn cards.
Read each sentence.
Decide if it needs a **.**, **!**, or **?**.
Glue a matching popcorn card at the end of
    the sentence.

1.   Do you like to eat popcorn

2.   I like butter and salt on my popcorn

3.   Does cheese popcorn taste good

4.   I could eat 100 bowls of popcorn in a day

5.   I like to eat popcorn at the movies

6.   My favorite kind of popcorn is caramel corn

7.   When will the popcorn be ready

8.   Oh my! I can't believe all of the popcorn is gone

9.   Wow! That popcorn is really hot

10. How much popcorn is left

Bonus Box: On the back of this sheet, write a story about
a magic popcorn popper. Remember to use correct punctuation.

?   ?   ?   ?   .   .   .   !   !   !

52 Name _____

A Kernel Of Truth

Read each group of words.
Color the popcorn beside the best ending.

1. Sam bought a ticket and some popcorn because

   (N) he will watch a movie.

   (C) he will watch a TV show at home.

2. Lin packed a suitcase because

   (H) she is going to the mall.

   (G) she is going on a trip.

3. Mark took out flour, sugar, and eggs because

   (L) he will draw.

   (V) he will bake.

4. Mia put on knee pads, elbow pads, and a helmet because

   (T) she is going skateboarding.

   (U) she is going swimming.

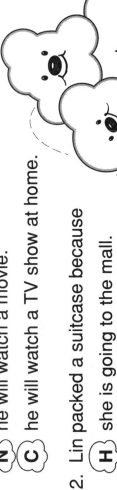

5. Tina will run to first base because

   (S) she struck out.

   (P) she got a hit.

6. Clay's friends will play games, eat cake, and give him gifts because

   (R) it is Clay's birthday.

   (D) Clay is sick.

7. Adam and Emily will buy bait and pack a lunch because

   (O) they are going to the library.

   (M) they are going fishing.

8. Bill is writing a list of things he needs because

   (F) he is going to the store.

   (E) he is going to read a book.

Why did Santa plant a garden full of popcorn? To solve the riddle, look at each piece of popcorn that is not colored. Write its letter above the matching number.

___ ___   ___ ___   ___ ___ ___ ___   ___ ___ ___ ___ ,   ___ ___ ___ ___   ___ ___ ___ !
 5   7   2   8   1   7   4   3   6   1   7   4   8   2   7   8   2   7   8

Name _____

Popcorn Place Value

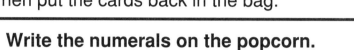

Cut apart the cards.
Place them in a small brown bag.
For each set of questions, take three cards from the bag.
Complete the work in the box.
Then put the cards back in the bag.

Write the numerals on the popcorn.

1. What is the **largest** number that you can make with these numerals? _____

2. Write it in expanded notation. _____ + _____ + _____

3. What is the **smallest** number that you can make? _____

4. Write it in expanded notation. _____ + _____ + _____

Write the numerals on the popcorn.

5. What is the **largest** number that you can make with these numerals? _____

6. Write it in expanded notation. _____ + _____ + _____

7. What is the **smallest** number that you can make? _____

8. Write it in expanded notation. _____ + _____ + _____

Write the numerals on the popcorn.

9. What is the **largest** number that you can make with these numerals? _____

10. Write it in expanded notation. _____ + _____ + _____

11. What is the **smallest** number that you can make? _____

12. Write it in expanded notation. _____ + _____ + _____

| 0 | 1 | 2 | 3 | 4 | 5 | 6 | 7 | 8 | 9 |

Plenty Of Popcorn

Read the words.
For each bowl, color the popcorn words that rhyme with the word on the bowl.

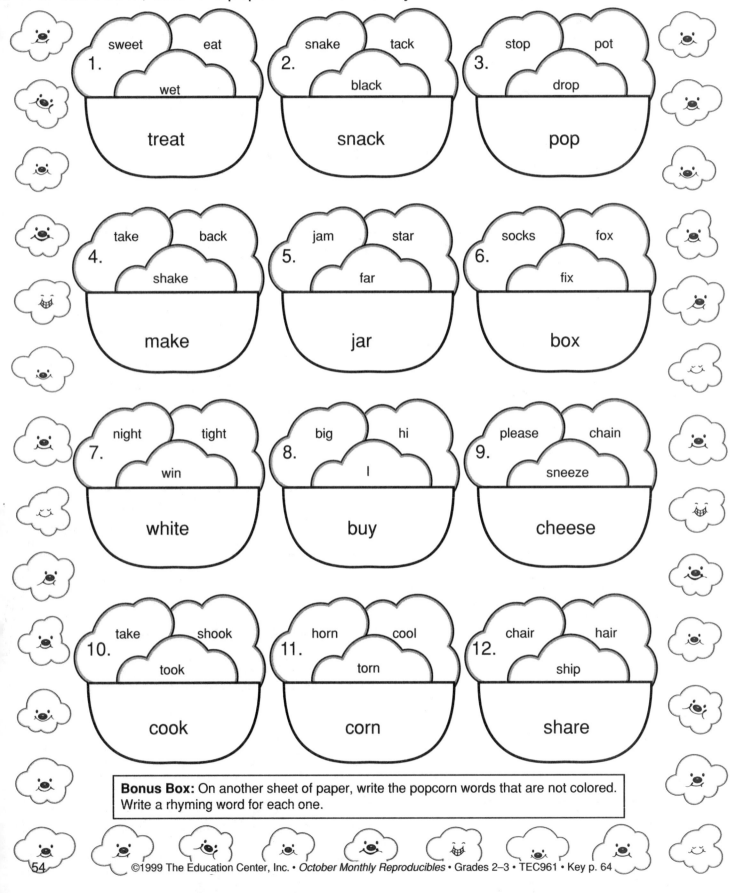

1. sweet   eat   wet   **treat**

2. snake   tack   black   **snack**

3. stop   pot   drop   **pop**

4. take   back   shake   **make**

5. jam   star   far   **jar**

6. socks   fox   fix   **box**

7. night   tight   win   **white**

8. big   hi   I   **buy**

9. please   chain   sneeze   **cheese**

10. take   shook   took   **cook**

11. horn   cool   torn   **corn**

12. chair   hair   ship   **share**

Bonus Box: On another sheet of paper, write the popcorn words that are not colored.
Write a rhyming word for each one.

NATIONAL COOKIE MONTH

It's cookie time! Celebrate one of America's favorite treats during October—National Cookie Month. Use these freshly baked activities and reproducibles to fill your classroom with the aroma of cookie fun!

Fresh Story Ideas

Encourage your students to bake up some hot new stories with this sweet idea! First duplicate a desired number of cookie patterns (page 56) on tan construction paper. Cut out the cookies; then program each one with a different writing prompt, such as the following:

- A Day In The Life Of A Cookie
- Oh, no! There are new cookies moving into the cookie jar!
- How The Cookie Escaped From The Hungry Children

Next, place the programmed cookies in a cookie jar. Each day, have a different student take a prompt from the jar and read it to the class. Instruct each student to write a story that focuses on the prompt. No doubt your creative authors will be eager to share their sweet cookie stories!

Gourmet Cookie Shop

With this stop at the cookie shop, youngsters work cooperatively to count change! Divide your class into pairs and give each twosome a copy of page 57. Provide each pair with a die, a green crayon, and play-money coins (15 pennies, 3 nickels, 3 dimes, 3 quarters, and 2 half-dollars). Partners will work together to earn money for a "gourmet cookie" surprise.

To play the game, each partner in turn rolls the die and places the corresponding number of pennies in the appropriate column on her activity sheet. If possible, she then trades the pennies for equivalent coins. Play continues in a like manner until the student pair has accumulated two 50-cent pieces. Then students color a dollar bill on their activity sheet. They clear the board and play again until they have earned a total of two dollars with which to "buy" two cookie homework passes (page 56). Students will love this sweet no-homework treat!

What is your favorite cookie?

Chocolate Chip	Peanut Butter	Oatmeal Raisin	Sugar
Mac			Bobby
Morgan			Lauren
Tyler	Darius		Darren
Michelle	Leigh	Jamar	Tanya

Sweet Statistics

Your youngsters will love this delicious graphing idea! Create a graph similar to the one shown on a large piece of bulletin-board paper; then display it in an easily accessible area. Purchase four different kinds of cookies and cut the cookies into small sample pieces. Label and place the samples in four different stations in your room. Duplicate the cookie pattern on page 56 and give one copy to each student. Divide students into small groups and have them visit each station to taste the cookies. Next have each youngster color and personalize his paper cookie as desired, cut it out, and tape it onto the graph section that shows his favorite cookie. Then ask each student to write a paragraph that explains the data on the graph. Oh, what scrumptious fun!

Books That Cook

A Cow, A Bee, A Cookie, And Me by Meredith Hooper (Kingfisher, 1997)
Chicken Soup For Little Souls: The New Kid And The Cookie Thief by Lisa McCourt (Health Communications, Inc.; 1998)
Young Cam Jansen And The Missing Cookie by David A. Adler (Viking, 1996)

Patterns

Use the cookie with "Sweet Statistics" and "Fresh Story Ideas" on page 55.
Use the coupons with "Gourmet Cookie Shop" on page 55.

©1999 The Education Center, Inc.

You're A Smart Cookie!

This cookie coupon is good for one homework assignment!

Name _____ Date _____

Assignment _____

©1999 The Education Center, Inc. • *October Monthly Reproducibles* • Grades 2–3 • TEC961

You're A Smart Cookie!

This cookie coupon is good for one homework assignment!

Name _____ Date _____

Assignment _____

©1999 The Education Center, Inc. • *October Monthly Reproducibles* • Grades 2–3 • TEC961

©1999 The Education Center, Inc. • *October Monthly Reproducibles* • Grades 2–3 • TEC961

Names_____

The Gourmet Cookie Shop

Follow your teacher's directions to buy a surprise from the Gourmet Cookie Shop.

Pennies	Nickels	Dimes	Quarters	Half-Dollars

Note To The Teacher: Use with "Gourmet Cookie Shop" on page 55.

The "Un-fortune-ate" Cookies

These poor fortune cookies can't get their fortunes until they are corrected. On each fortune, circle each letter that needs to be capitalized. Color each fortune cookie as you use its letter.

Fortunes

Your lucky month is october.	your lucky numbers for the month are 3, 6, 9, and 12.	good things will happen in your life.
listening to your teacher will pay off.	If you study hard in school, you will land on easy street.	Your lucky day is thursday.
You're going to become a hollywood star!	making others smile will bring you a nice reward.	The good-luck name of the month is steve.
You'll have a great time learning about national cookie month.	mr. sunshine will brighten your days.	
Your teacher is proud of you. keep up the good work!		

A person who makes delicious cookies is called a

_ _ _ _ _ _ _ !

To solve the puzzle, unscramble the letters on the five cookies that you did not color.

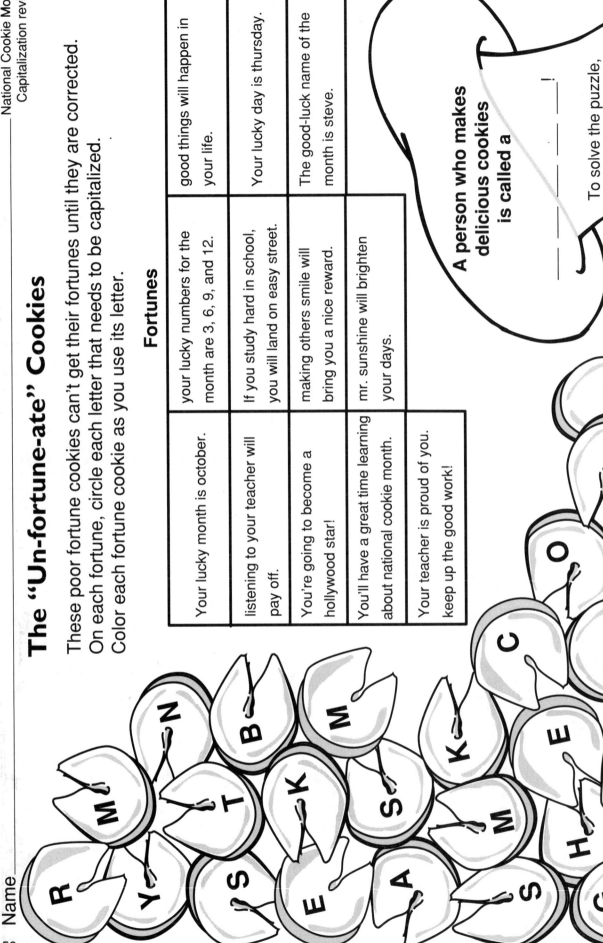

Bonus Box: On the back of this sheet, write three rules for using capital letters.

COMPUTER LEARNING MONTH

Have your youngsters take a "byte" out of technology with these nifty ideas for Computer Learning Month!

Computer Care

Teach students proper care of computers *and* review consonant blends with this trendy tachistoscope! Give each youngster a construction-paper copy of page 60. To make a tachistoscope, the student writes in each program-strip blank either *dr* or *cl* so that each sentence makes sense. Then he colors the remaining pieces and signs his name on the monitor. Next the student cuts out each pattern and carefully cuts along the dotted lines to make slits. He cuts two lengths of yarn to represent cables, then tapes one end of a yarn length to the back of the hard drive and the other end to the back of the monitor. In a similar manner, he links the keyboard to the monitor with the second length of yarn. The student puts his floppy disk in the slit on his hard drive and glues it in place.

To use his paper computer, the student inserts the prepared program strip into the monitor and displays the title. Then he presses the return key and pulls up the strip to show the first computer care tip. After he reads it, the youngster presses the return key and slides the strip up to reveal the second tip. He repeats this process until he has read all the tips. Now, that's one way to monitor computer responsibility!

Computer Fact Or Mouse's Opinion?

No doubt your youngsters will have fun pointing out facts and opinions with this computer-related activity! Give each student a copy of the reproducible on page 61. Instruct her to read and cut out the sentence strips at the bottom of the sheet, then glue the facts onto the computer monitor and the opinions onto the keyboard. Next have each student color and cut out the three patterns. Have the student use two brads to attach the arm and tail cutouts to the mouse where indicated. Then pair students. Have each youngster, in turn, carefully use his mouse's arm for a pointer as he reads the facts to his partner. Then ask him to use the tail for a pointer as he reads the opinions. You won't mind these mice in the classroom—and that's a fact!

Patterns
Use with "Computer Care" on page 59.

Monitor

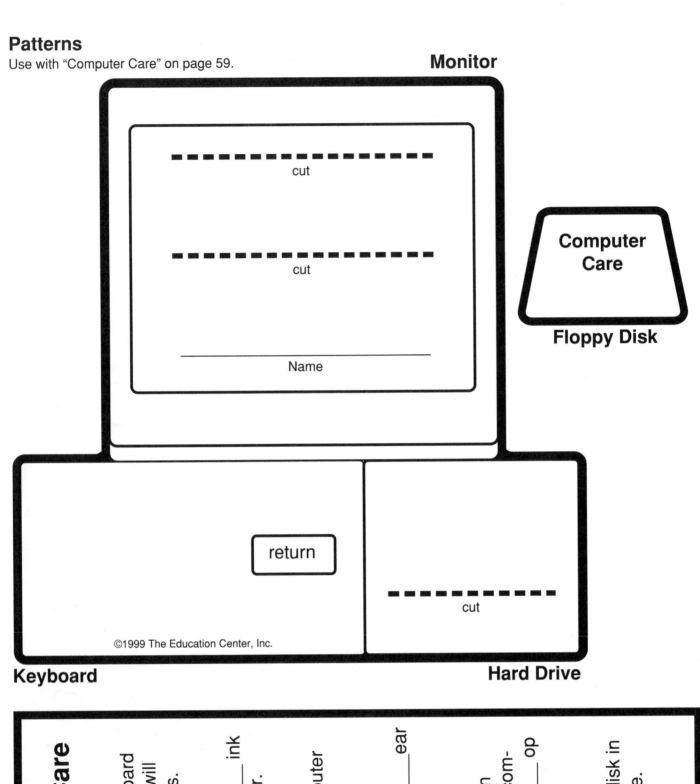

cut

cut

Name

Computer Care

Floppy Disk

return

cut

©1999 The Education Center, Inc.

Keyboard

Hard Drive

Computer Care

1. Keep the keyboard _____ ean. Dust will _____ og the keys.

2. Do not eat or _____ ink at the computer.

3. Keep the computer _____ y.

4. Keep the area _____ ear of _____ utter.

5. Do not _____ own around at the computer. Do not _____ op any part of it.

6. Put only your disk in the disk _____ ive.

Program Strip

Facts

Opinions

A computer can help us get work done.	Everyone should own a computer.
Computers come in many sizes and colors.	You press the keys on the keyboard to type.
A computer is the best tool for getting work done.	A mouse is sometimes used with a computer.
You can play games on a computer.	The mouse is the most important part of the computer.
All computers should be gray.	Computers cost too much money.

Note To The Teacher: Use with "Computer Fact Or Mouse's Opinion?" on page 59.

Name _____

Mouse Match

Solve each problem.
For each computer mouse, find the real
   mouse with the same answer.
Color the matching mice the same color.
Use a different color for each pair of
   mice.

1. 534
  − 219

2. 319
  + 345

3. 876
  − 285

4. 172
  + 687

5. 896
  − 232

6. 193
  + 447

7. 544
  + 307

8. 119
  + 196

9. 409
  − 195

10. 270
  + 321

11. 991
  − 132

12. 733
  − 93

13. 958
  − 107

14. 217
  + 498

15. 119
  + 95

16. 897
  − 182

Answer Keys

Page 8
1. tiny
2. below
3. short
4. thin
5. noisy
6. empty
7. off
8. bent
9. stands
10. front

Page 9
1. 4
2. 12
3. 14
4. 16
5. 20
6. 19
7. 17
8. 15
9. 9
10. 7

Page 14
blue (soft *g*): giant, gem, giraffe
purple (hard *g*): goose, gate, gallop
yellow (soft *c*): cider, circle, cent
green (hard *c*): cake, coat, cow

Page 15
A. 12
B. 14
C. 18
D. 16
E. 15
F. 15
G. 13
H. 16
I. 13
J. 14
K. 18
L. 15
M. 18
N. 18
O. 17

Bonus Box: 16 (problem-solving strategies will vary)

Page 19

3 ax	3 bucket	1 rescue	3 spray
1 aid	2 boots	3 rope	2 smoky
2 alarm	1 best	2 rig	2 siren

4 pump	1 fire	2 chief	2 hack
2 pole	3 foam	1 captain	5 hydrant
3 protect	4 fumes	5 crew	3 hose
1 people	2 flames	4 company	2 helmet
		3 clue	1 hunt

3 emergency	4 special
5 extinguisher	5 walkie-talkie
2 dalmatian	1 mask
6 ladder	3 safety
4 equipment	2 nozzle
1 break	6 work

Page 20
Firefighters wait for the alarm to go off.
When the alarm goes off, the firefighters stop what they are doing.
The firefighters get on the truck quickly, and off it goes!
The firefighters fight the blaze with special equipment.
After the fire is out, firefighters clean and check their equipment.
The firefighters return to the station to wait for another call.

Page 23
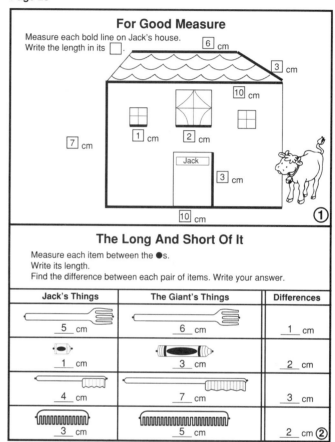

Page 24
1 cm: apple, salt
2 cm: butter, pie
3 cm: juice, carrot
4 cm: turkey, bread

Jack's house — 6 cm, 8 cm, 4 cm, 5 cm, 4 cm, 5 cm, 6 cm, 3 cm, 5 cm

How far did Jack travel in all? 46 cm

63

Answer Keys

Page 36

A. 29, 36, 42, 68
B. 10, 12, 34, 60
C. 18, 22, 78, 83
D. 29, 43, 50, 99
E. 17, 39, 87, 96
F. 16, 33, 56, 64

Page 40

△ A. 10, 15, 20, 25, 30, 35, 40, 45, 50
□ B. 6, 9, 12, 15, 18, 21, 24, 27, 30
○ C. 8, 10, 12, 14, 16, 18, 20, 22, 24
□ D. 18, 21, 24, 27, 30, 33, 36, 39, 42
△ E. 45, 50, 55, 60, 65, 70, 75, 80, 85
○ F. 34, 36, 38, 40, 42, 44, 46, 48, 50
○ G. 40, 42, 44, 46, 48, 50, 52, 54, 56
□ H. 30, 33, 36, 39, 42, 45, 48, 51, 54

Page 41

ch air	sh ort	wh isper	sh ade
sh ell	wh eels	th ought	ch ain
wh ile	ch arm	sh out	sh arp
th ing	wh iskers	th ird	ch art

1. sharp
2. whisper
3. third
4. short
5. chair
6. while
7. shout
8. wheels

Page 42

1. 3	7	9	5		4. 4	8	3	5
2. 8	6	10	4		5. 5	12	8	9
3. 9	4	11	8		6. 4	6	2	7

Page 46

1. little
2. fast
3. near
4. also
5. large
6. yell
7. whole
8. fantastic
9. delicious

Page 47

A. 5:00
B. 7:30
C. 11:30
D. 3:00
E. 8:30
F. 1:30
G. 4:00
H. 12:30

1. Clock E will have a ☆.
2. Clock G will have an X.
3. Clock B will have a △.

Page 48

1. 2/3
2. 3/4
3. 1/2
4. 1/4
5. 5/6
6. 2/3
7. 4/6
8. 3/4

For problems 9–12, answers will vary.

Page 51

1. ?
2. .
3. ?
4. !
5. .
6. .
7. ?
8. !
9. !
10. ?

Page 52

1. he will watch a movie.
2. she is going on a trip.
3. he will bake.
4. she is going skateboarding.
5. she got a hit.
6. it is Clay's birthday.
7. they are going fishing.
8. he is going to the store.

SO HE COULD HOE, HOE, HOE!

Page 54

1. sweet, eat
2. black, tack
3. stop, drop
4. take, shake
5. far, star
6. socks, fox
7. night, tight
8. I, hi
9. please, sneeze
10. took, shook
11. horn, torn
12. chair, hair

Bonus Box: Answers will vary.

Page 58

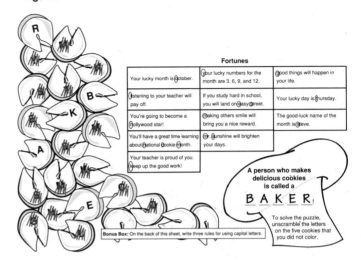

Fortunes

Your lucky month is October.	Your lucky numbers for the month are 3, 6, 9, and 12.	Good things will happen in your life.
Listening to your teacher will pay off.	If you study hard in school, you will land on Easy Street.	Your lucky day is Thursday.
You're going to become a Hollywood star!	Making others smile will bring you a nice reward.	The good-luck name of the month is Steve.
You'll have a great time learning about National Cookie Month.	Mr. Sunshine will brighten your days.	
Your teacher is proud of you. Keep up the good work!		

A person who makes delicious cookies is called a

B A K E R

To solve the puzzle, unscramble the letters on the five cookies that you did not color.

Bonus Box: On the back of this sheet, write three rules for using capital letters.

Page 61

(The order of answers may vary.)

Facts:

A computer can help us get work done.
Computers come in many sizes and colors.
You can play games on a computer.
You press the keys on the keyboard to type.
A mouse is sometimes used with a computer.

Opinions:

A computer is the best tool for getting work done.
All computers should be gray.
Everyone should own a computer.
The mouse is the most important part of the computer.
Computers cost too much money.

Page 62

1. 315
2. 664
3. 591
4. 859
5. 664
6. 640
7. 851
8. 315
9. 214
10. 591
11. 859
12. 640
13. 851
14. 715
15. 214
16. 715